# Positive Affirmations
## Journal With Writing Prompts

# Dedication

This Positive Affirmations For Women Journal is dedicated to all the women out there who want to empower themselves by using positive affirmations and document their findings in the process.

You are my inspiration for producing books and I'm honored to be a part of keeping all of your Positive Affirmations notes and records organized.

This journal notebook will help you record your details about your affirmations.

This journal will help make you dig deep and help you focus on the life you are living and the life you want to live. It will help you explore your self-love, your beliefs, your gratitude, your manifestations, the law of attraction, your mind set, self-confidence, happiness, truths, intents, your vision board ideas, success, your attitude, self-discovery and much, much more.

# How to Use this Book

The purpose of this book is to keep all of your Positive Affirmations notes all in one place. It will help keep you organized.

This Positive Affirmations For Women Journal will allow you to accurately document every detail about your self discovery experience. It's a great way to chart your course through your daily affirmations.

Here are examples of the prompts for you to fill in and write about your experience in this book:

1. Whom Do I Want To Become?

2. Today I Affirm

3. Today I Am Proud When I

4. What Fills Me Up With Meaning & Passion

5. Things I Can Change To Be My Higher Self

6. I Forgive Myself For

7. 20 Things That Make Me Smile

8. Fears That Are Stopping Me From Moving Forward

9. How I Want To Be Remembered

10. The One Thing I Look Forward To Every Day

And much, much more!

## What am I at this moment?

## Who do I want to become?

# I Am Happy...

Some things I did well today:

- ❑ _____
- ❑ _____
- ❑ _____
- ❑ _____
- ❑ _____

Something good that happened to me today was:

- ❑ _____
- ❑ _____
- ❑ _____
- ❑ _____
- ❑ _____

Today I affirm:

_____

_____

_____

_____

# Today, I am proud when I...

What fills me up with meaning and passion?

Things I can change in order to be my higher self...

## Create your own affirmations

1. 
2. 
3. 
4. 
5. 
6. 
7. 
8. 
9. 
10. 
11. 
12. 
13. 
14. 
15. 
16. 
17. 
18. 
19. 
20.

## How has God blessed me today?

## I know exactly what I need to do to achieve success...

*I forgive myself for...*

_____
_____
_____
_____
_____
_____
_____

*Self-love means...*

_____
_____
_____
_____
_____
_____
_____

## 20 things that make me smile

1. 
2. 
3. 
4. 
5. 
6. 
7. 
8. 
9. 
10. 
11. 
12. 
13. 
14. 
15. 
16. 
17. 
18. 
19. 
20.

## Fears that are stopping you from moving forward...

## How are you showing up for yourself?

*Today I affirm:*

_____

_____

_____

_____

*Draw anything that comes to mind relating to "Positive"*

*Today I affirm:*

_____

_____

_____

_____

*Draw anything that comes to mind relating to "Happiness"*

Today I affirm:

_____
_____
_____
_____

Draw anything that comes to mind relating to "Success"

*Today I affirm:*

_____

_____

_____

_____

*Draw anything that comes to mind relating to "Self-love"*

# Today, I will/have accomplished...

- [ ] _____
- [ ] _____
- [ ] _____
- [ ] _____
- [ ] _____
- [ ] _____
- [ ] _____
- [ ] _____
- [ ] _____
- [ ] _____

How I feel after accomplishing the things above:

_____
_____
_____
_____

*How I want to be remembered...*

*The one thing I look forward to every day... Why?*

*What is your favorite personality trait?*

*Where do you see yourself in 10 years?*

*What is your one word of intention today?*

_____
_____
_____
_____
_____
_____
_____
_____

*5 things that truly make me happy are... And why?*

_____
_____
_____
_____
_____
_____
_____
_____

## 5 things I want to rearrange in my life

1. _____

2. _____

3. _____

4. _____

5. _____


## What excites me?

_____
_____
_____
_____
_____
_____
_____
_____
_____
_____
_____

# 5 traits that make you a good person

1. _____
2. _____
3. _____
4. _____
5. _____

# I deserve happiness because...

_____

_____

_____

_____

_____

_____

_____

_____

_____

# Write a "Thank You" letter to your body for all it is capable of

# Write a "Thank You" letter to yourself for all that you have achieved so far

*Look at your hands. Write something positive about them.*

*Describe your "best day ever".*

# Illustrate your "Best Day Ever"

What do you look and feel like when you are most confident?

_____
_____
_____
_____
_____
_____
_____

Ways I can step out of old bad habits...

_____
_____
_____
_____
_____
_____
_____
_____

*Dig deep. What do I want to learn about myself?*

_____

_____

_____

_____

_____

_____

_____

*What is something you do better than your peers?*

_____

_____

_____

_____

_____

_____

_____

## What do you want more of in your life?

_____
_____
_____
_____
_____
_____
_____
_____

## My favorite quote... Why?

_____
_____
_____
_____
_____
_____
_____
_____
_____

# Free Write (anything that is positive)

# Positive changes that happened to me in the last year...

*If you were a flower, what kind would you be? Why?*

_____
_____
_____
_____
_____
_____

*Illustrate the kind of flower you chose. Don't forget to color.*

*What would make your teenage self proud of you now?*

*Describe yourself through the eyes of a loved one.*

## 20 things that I'm grateful for this week

1.
2.
3.
4.
5.
6.
7.
8.
9.
10.
11.
12.
13.
14.
15.
16.
17.
18.
19.
20.

# How to make next month a great month?

*My wildest lifetime goal is: _____*
*I can achieve this by...*

## Acts of kindness I've done for the week

1.
2.
3.
4.
5.
6.
7.
8.
9.
10.
11.
12.
13.
14.
15.
16.
17.
18.
19.
20.

*I love myself...*

How am I living to my full potential?

*I radiate positive energy by...*

*I am getting better everyday by...*

## How I can spread joy in random & beautiful ways

1.
2.
3.
4.
5.
6.
7.
8.
9.
10.
11.
12.
13.
14.
15.
16.
17.
18.
19.
20.

## I think like a winner by...

## How am I able to solve problems creatively?

How can I turn obstacles and challenges in to learning opportunities?

How can I see the bright side in all situations?

*I am a wonderful person because...*

*I am important because...*

*I am loved because...*

*I can do anything I put my mind into because...*

*I am strong because...*

_____
_____
_____
_____
_____
_____
_____

*I am hopeful because...*

_____
_____
_____
_____
_____
_____
_____

*I make things happen by...*

*Everything I do turns into success because...*

*I am lucky to be me because...*

_____
_____
_____
_____
_____
_____
_____

*Today was a good day because...*

_____
_____
_____
_____
_____
_____
_____

## Positive habits I want to work on...

1.
2.
3.
4.
5.
6.
7.
8.
9.
10.
11.
12.
13.
14.
15.
16.
17.
18.
19.
20.

# Positive thoughts I have about myself

# Positive thoughts I have about myself

One thing I'll never regret is...

_____
_____
_____
_____
_____
_____
_____

A sentence that stopped me in my tracks and changed my outlook was...

_____
_____
_____
_____
_____
_____
_____

The quality I admire most in others is...

The best advice I could give to a younger me

## Activities I do because I love myself

1.
2.
3.
4.
5.
6.
7.
8.
9.
10.
11.
12.
13.
14.
15.
16.
17.
18.
19.
20.

# The simplest things that make me happy

1. 
2. 
3. 
4. 
5. 
6. 
7. 
8. 
9. 
10. 
11. 
12. 
13. 
14. 
15. 
16. 
17. 
18. 
19. 
20.

*I am a problem solver...*

*Today, I succeeded at...*

# Draw about how you are feeling today

*The person I admire is:* _____
*What qualities do I share with this person?*

*8 favorite self-confidence quotes to reference on a bad day*

1. _____
   _____

2. _____
   _____

3. _____
   _____

4. _____
   _____

5. _____
   _____

6. _____
   _____

7. _____
   _____

8. _____
   _____

*What is one compliment you struggle to accept?*

*How I can reframe the way I talk to myself to be more confident*

# Things I would do if I weren't afraid

1.

Why?

2.

Why?

3.

Why?

4.

Why?

5.

Why?

6.

Why?

7.

Why?

Best compliment I've ever received. Do you agree?

What can I learn from my biggest triumph?

# My confidence building playlist

1.

2.

3.

4.

5.

6.

7.

8.

9.

10.

*I feel amazing when...*

_____
_____
_____
_____
_____
_____
_____

*My greatest strength or strengths are...*

_____
_____
_____
_____
_____
_____
_____

*How can I turn my weaknesses into something positive?*

*I manage stress by...*

## I pamper myself by...

1.

2.

3.

4.

5.

6.

7.

8.

9.

10.

# What are you thinking of right now?

# People in my life who make me feel loved

1.

Why?

2.

Why?

3.

Why?

4.

Why?

5.

Why?

## My motto in life

## Why and how do I live it daily?

# Things I can do to make a positive impact on people

1.

2.

3.

4.

5.

6.

7.

8.

9.

10.

# Things I can do to make a positive impact on the environment

1.

2.

3.

4.

5.

6.

7.

8.

9.

10.

# I am grateful for... Because....

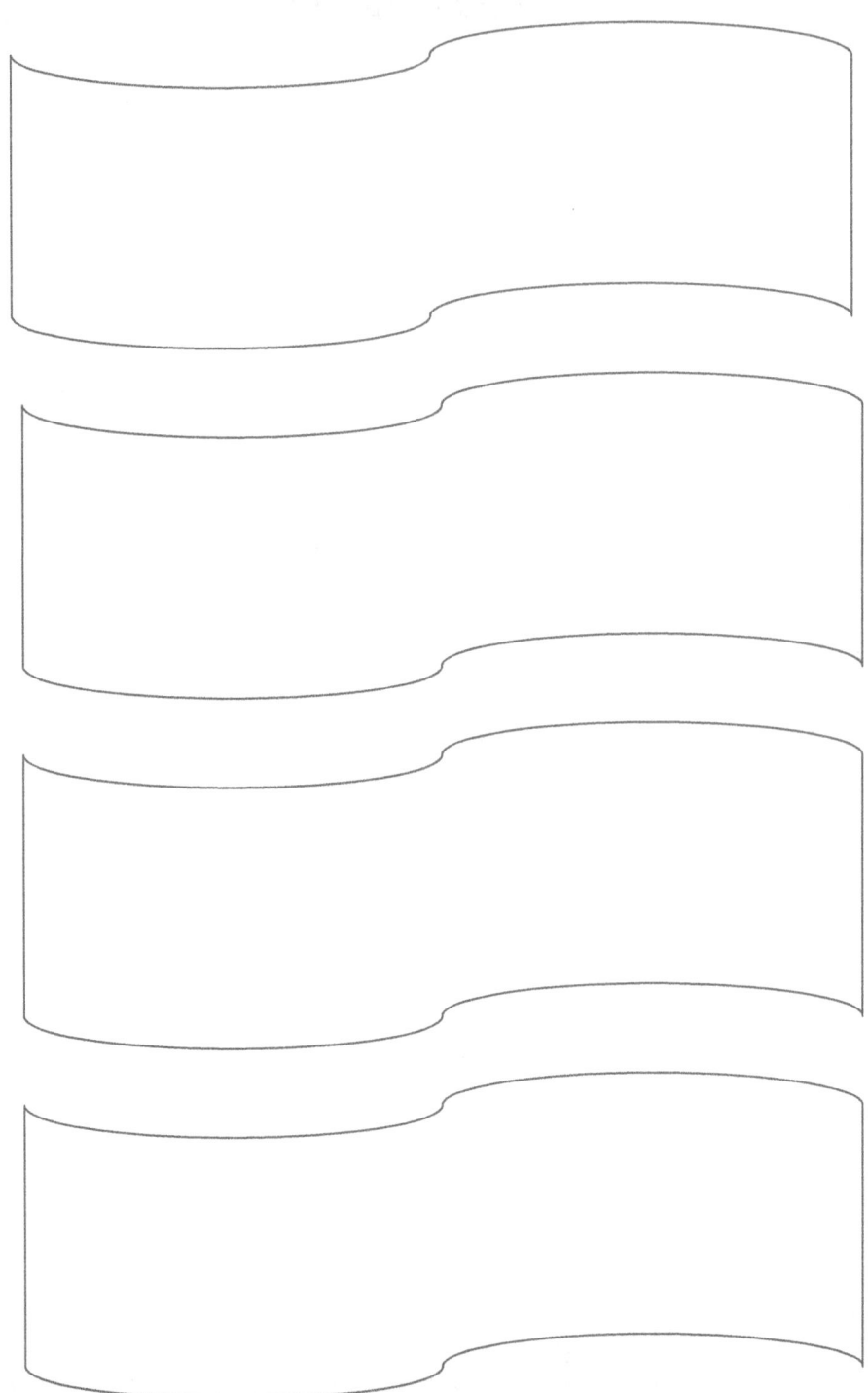

# I am grateful for... Because....

*Daily opportunities that I take whole-heartedly...*

_____
_____
_____
_____
_____
_____
_____
_____

*Daily opportunities that I take for granted...*

_____
_____
_____
_____
_____
_____
_____
_____

*I am beautiful because...*

_____
_____
_____
_____
_____
_____
_____
_____

*I stay motivated by...*

_____
_____
_____
_____
_____
_____
_____
_____

What do I need to be content?

The one thing I dream of doing is...

# Write a poem that describes the feeling of self-confidence

*What do you see when you look in the mirror?*

_____
_____
_____
_____
_____
_____
_____
_____

*Does confidence relate to happiness? Why or why not?*

_____
_____
_____
_____
_____
_____
_____
_____

*Why is it important to congratulate people who do well?*

*How does it feel to be congratulated? Share your experience.*

# Give yourself a special award

*Describe the award you've given yourself. Why did you choose to give this award?*

# What does it feel like when someone recognizes something you worked hard to do?

*The greatest feeling I've ever had...*

*Write about your favorite intellectual quality*

*What kinds of things hurt self-esteem?*

___

*How can you discourage things that hurt self-esteem?*

How can I sympathize with others when they're feeling down?

Today, I seek peace by...

*Today, I will slow down and enjoy the moment by...*

*Write a prayer for optimism*

## Hum a tune that will give positive vibes

## Hard things make me stronger by...

# Things that make me laugh

1.

Why?

2.

Why?

3.

Why?

4.

Why?

5.

Why?

# Things that make me laugh

1.

Why?

2.

Why?

3.

Why?

4.

Why?

5.

Why?

## Why is laughter good for my health?

## Is staying fit a good way to be more confident?

*Ways I can stay fit & healthy*

---

*Write a memory that you cherish the most*

*Practice makes progress. What are you practicing on to be better at?*

---

*Today, I will do what is right, not what is easy. What did you do?*

*What book have you read that has a positive impact on your life?*

*Write about your favorite places.*

# Yearly events that bring happiness

1.

Why?

2.

Why?

3.

Why?

4.

Why?

5.

Why?

# Yearly events that bring happiness

1.

Why?

2.

Why?

3.

Why?

4.

Why?

5.

Why?

# Top 5 favorite movies that inspire positivity

1.

Why?

2.

Why?

3.

Why?

4.

Why?

5.

Why?

# Write something positive about each of the seasons below

Winter

Spring

Summer

Fall

# Something positive that you saw each day of the week

**Monday**

**Tuesday**

**Wednesday**

**Thursday**

**Friday**

**Saturday**

**Sunday**

*I love my job because...*

*Positive changes in me I've noticed compared to 5 years ago*

## I will avoid negativity by...

## How can I win the day?

*I am perfect because...*

 

*I am worthy because...*

www.ingramcontent.com/pod-product-compliance
Lightning Source LLC
Chambersburg PA
CBHW071408080526
44587CB00017B/3209